THE *Entrepreneurial* CAT

JAZZIE THE CAT
& MARY HESSLER, Ph.D.

THE
Entrepreneurial
CAT

13 Ways to Transform Your Business Life
by

JAZZIE THE CAT
& MARY HESSLER, Ph.D.

ILLUSTRATIONS
BY KOTOPOULIS

Jazzie Publishing
Tampa, Florida

The Entrepreneurial Cat is published by Jazzie Publishing
ISBN 0-9660318-0-6

For permission write to:

Jazzie Publishing
Mary Hessler, Ph.D.
2914 Alline Ave.
Tampa, FL 33611

Art direction & typesetting
Drawing Board Studios, Land-O-Lakes, FL
813-996-1900

For prices and quantities regarding ordering this book or any
®Jazzie the Cat merchandise call the publisher at 813-831-9500
or e-mail: MaryHess@aol.com

First edition 1 2 3 4 5

This book was manufactured in China

TABLE OF CONTENTS

1
DO WHAT COMES NATURALLY

2
BE CURIOUS AND FIND THE RIGHT NICHE

3
MAKE THE LEAP

4
FOLLOW YOUR INSTINCTS

5
CLEAN YOUR LITTER BOX

6
SIT IN THE WINDOW AND WATCH

7
MEANDER AND EXPLORE

8
TAKE NAPS

9
BE PURRSISTENT

10
WASH OFTEN

11
GROOM THOSE WHO GROOM YOU

12
FOCUS WHILE HUNTING

13
BALANCE SKILLFULLY

APPENDIX
CATS-CAN!

DEDICATION

This book is dedicated to Sheba and
Jasper for their love and support

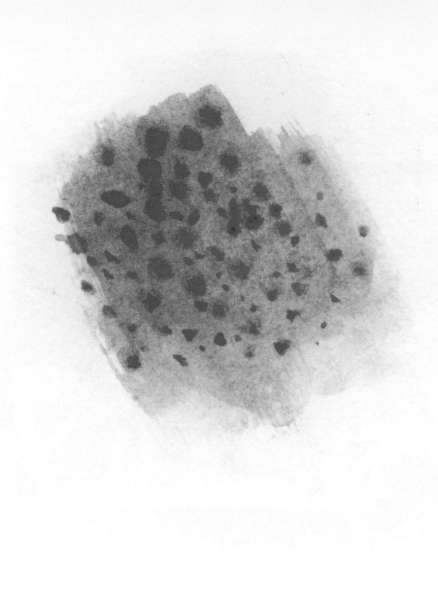

PREFACE

For over ten years, I depended on a major consulting firm for my paycheck. I saw myself as an entrepreneur because, as a management consultant, I was responsible for developing my own customer base. In retrospect, I realize that my employer was my safety net. Although I took risks, I never made the leap of faith that all true entrepreneurs make. Never, that is, until the day a prospective client asked whether I'd be interested in running a start-up medical device company.

In consulting, as in life, there are bridesmaids and there are brides. Helping others down the corporate aisle, I was always the bridesmaid. Finally, here was a suitor with a proposal that I wasn't about to let slip away. I took the plunge. I accepted the challenge. I imagined it wouldn't be long before I'd be looking at myself on the cover of *Inc. Magazine*. Talk about your short honeymoons. In four months, the company's product was taken off the market. The company was finished and so was I; that's what I thought at the time anyway.

Out of a job and anxious for a career change, I started to work on freelance projects for past clients while I reassessed my own life. Before long, I had developed a full-time consulting practice. I became an entrepreneur by accident. My two cats, Sheba and Jasper, were my closest companions as I worked alone, out of my home. They were my inspiration in those frantic and frightening times. Through their affection and example, I learned how to be a successful entrepreneur. For the lessons they taught me, I dedicate this book to them. Sheba and Jasper are "Jazzie," the Cat with Attitude.

Mary Hessler

Mary Hessler
Tampa, Florida 1997

FOREWORD

Let me introduce myself

Let's be perfectly clear from the beginning: I'm just your average intelligent, beautiful, lovable, luxurious, low-maintenance feline. But enough about *me*.

I really want to tell you about my Person. She's loving. She's lots of fun. She's also very dependable—a good provider. But when she started our business last year, she forgot what she was working for, about the important things in life—mainly me!

At first, business was great! She sat at her desk, typing on her computer and talking on the telephone. I tickled her bare legs with my silky coat. My food bowl was never empty and my litter box was always clean. When I'd kiss her toes with my cold, wet nose, she'd reach down and scratch me between my ears.

But suddenly, life changed. Things started to get out of hand. My Person got very busy and really nervous about all the commitments she made. Silence replaced the shower songs I loved before breakfast. She started keeping long hours and darting from thing to thing. People and phone calls would get her off-track and she didn't take any quiet time to figure out what to do next.

My bowl was frequently empty and I'd have to remind her to fill it up. My litter box got dirty more often than it got cleaned. For the first time in my nine lives, I hadn't a clue what to do. This was serious.

Catastrophe loomed.

Then one day, as I rolled in my sunbeam watching my poor, struggling Person type and talk, talk and type, it hit me! **Cats take charge of their lives**. Persons rarely do. I made a command decision: I would have to help her. So I scratched out a cat-a-log for her, and as it turns out, for other budding entrepreneurs.

HEY, THIS IS A GOOD ONE
GREAT!
WOW! THIS WORKS
RIGHT ON
AH, PURRFECT
OKAY

If you're thinking about becoming an entrepreneur, if you are one, or if you just want to be more successful in your business life, listen to me. Hear what I have to say.

1

DO WHAT COMES NATURALLY

Cats certainly don't worry about what others think. Part of our not inconsiderable charm is in our "cattitude." We delight in our independence. So should you delight in yours.

Pick a business or career that lets you express your talents. Discover what you love to do. Do only that, and do it well.

And if you can't succeed without unraveling yarn and fetching sticks, unravel the yarn. Then delegate: find a dog to fetch the sticks.

2

BE CURIOUS AND
FIND THE RIGHT NICHE

Cats prowl for opportunity. We explore our territory by sight and scent. We squeeze into nooks and crannies other creatures wouldn't consider. Want to rearrange the furniture? Go right ahead. We'll adapt to the new room. We'll make it ours.

And so should you. Take your product or service and explore old ground as if it were new. Constantly look for ways to fill your customer's needs and to innovate within the shifting furniture of your market. Curiosity never killed a cat. In fact, we thrive on it.

3

MAKE THE LEAP

Dogs trot. Cats leap.

Cats gauge the distance we want to cross, then strategically position ourselves to spring with confidence. We are fearless. But I've learned the hard way that fear of failure can keep even the most successful Persons from leaping to new heights.

Gauge your distance. Position yourself. Then, *leap*! For goodness' sake. Be confident. And if you miss, believe you'll land on your feet.

4

FOLLOW YOUR INSTINCTS

How do cats pick precisely the right moment to pounce on a mouse? How do we know when our Person needs the solace only a furry, purring cat can provide?

We follow our instincts.

When you're faced with difficult decisions, like whether to take on a new project or start a business, don't just weigh the pros and cons. Before you make your move, listen to the meowing within!

5

CLEAN YOUR LITTER BOX

Cats demand fresh starts. To avoid a dirty litter box, we'll substitute anything—the carpet in your living room, the mattress on your bed, the papers in your briefcase.

Don't get so caught up in your daily pursuits that you forget to start over fresh. Take time regularly to tidy up your stuff. Let go of the past. Purge your disappointments, your lost opportunities, your old files—anything you don't need now.

Like cats, live in the present. Clean out the old and begin again. It will make a big difference in your business, and in your life.

6

SIT IN THE WINDOW AND WATCH

Cats devote hours to sitting in a window and watching the world go by. If a bug, a bird, or a dog enters our backyard jungle, we're poised to pounce because we've studied the terrain so thoroughly. Furthermore, cats have the power to remove ourselves from a situation and observe without getting emotionally attached.

Sit apart from the emotional investment you have in your business or your work. Observe your environment closely and with detachment. You'll improve your strategy and your game.

7

MEANDER AND EXPLORE

Wherever cats go, we make it a point to enjoy the trip. We learn about our territory by meandering and exploring. We pleasure in the discoveries we make along the way. Whatever path we take, you can be sure it's the right one.

Cats stay open. We don't waste our energy judging ourselves or the other creatures we meet along the way. We trust that things come together in the end. Nature has a way of self-organizing. Your life does too—if you let it.

Don't worry about straying off the beaten path in business. Never lose your wanderlust. Take a new path.

Get more out of your work and your life.

8

TAKE NAPS

Ever wonder why cats sleep in so many different positions? When we're catnapping, we're considering all the possibilities. We hunt in our dreams to make ourselves better hunters when we're awake.

Catnap occasionally. Dreaming improves creativity, concentration, and performance. It opens your eyes to other ideas and alternatives. If you're getting stuck and you can't see things from a new angle, take a nap and get an original perspective.

9

BE PURRSISTENT

We'll taste new food, but we'll make no secret of the fact if it isn't to our liking. We walk away from unappetizing bowls with style and grace—our dignity always in place. Cats don't compromise.

Neither should you. Discover what you like and what you don't. Respect yourself. Be assertive and purrsistent about your preferences. It's critical to reaching your goals.

Walk away from opportunities that don't meet your standards. And, like a cat, do it with class!

10

WASH OFTEN

It may be the same fur coat, but we're happy to wear it as long as it's clean and fresh. Washing renews us: body, mind, and spirit. Nothing feels better than a bath.

Renew yourself with a massage, a quiet meditation, a brisk walk or a vacation. A bubble bath doesn't have to take a lot of time. You can refresh yourself a little here and there, like closing your eyes to relax before your next appointment. Make time for the basic pleasures in life. It will help you to stay relaxed in the dog-eat-dog world of business!

11

GROOM THOSE
WHO GROOM YOU

Whoever says cats are aloof is barking up the wrong tree. We're social animals. We groom friends and even mere acquaintances, helping each other reach the spots we can't reach alone.

Be independent, but don't isolate yourself. Find others you can trust, and build relationships. Be a catalyst—groom those who would look less sleek without you. By helping others to be at their best, you'll achieve your best, too.

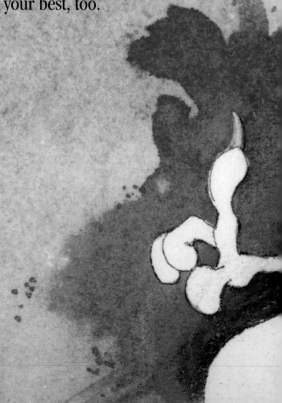

12

FOCUS WHILE HUNTING

Cats stalk their prey with focus. Nothing else exists except the bird we're hunting. Hours can pass while we wait for that bug to crawl out from under the curtain. We're ready. We're committed.
That bug is doomed.

Concentration is the key. We keep our minds clear and our bodies aligned. Unless there's a temporary crisis (like being chased by a you-know-what), we devote our energy to the hunt. Don't get distracted by the phone, other people, or competing demands.

Pick your priority. Be relentless.

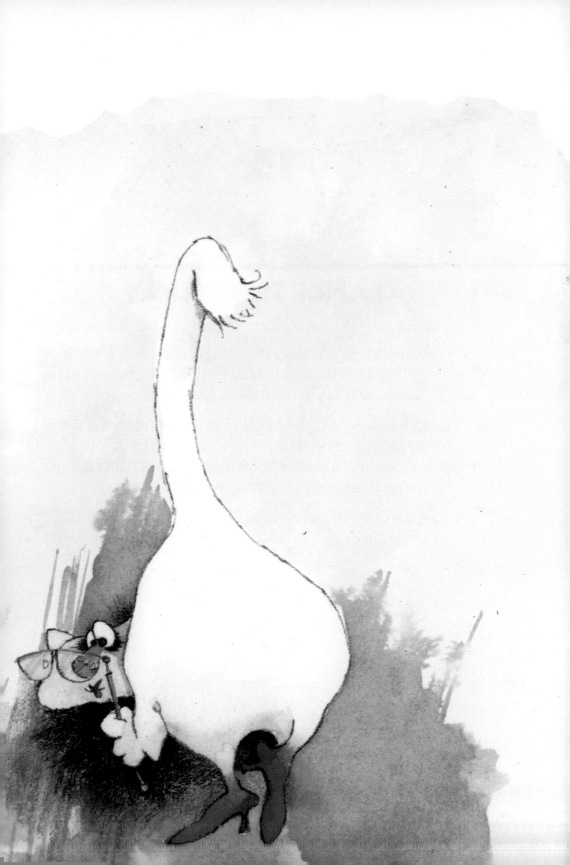

13

BALANCE SKILLFULLY

Cats stay on top of things. No matter how steep the challenge, our focus keeps our equilibrium in the midst of chaos. Even if we happen to slip and fall, we land on all fours.

Don't let your business concerns or your personal problems trip you up. Understand how important it is to blend every part of your life. Find ways to deliciously mix the critical ingredients-hunting, kittens, purring, sunbeams, napping, mind and spirit.

Balancing skillfully makes for a fulfilling and happy life!

FIND YOUR PLACE IN THE SUN

Once you've put these 13 principles into practice, you'll be content.

Your business will begin to grow.

You'll feel more relaxed, and you'll enjoy life more.

When cats are content, we find a ray of sunshine and stretch in it to rest. Even a Person can find a place in the sun. Celebrate and feel the glow of satisfaction that comes when you've done what comes naturally, made that leap, and balanced your life.

Meow for now,

Jazzie

CATS-CAN!

I. Do What Comes Naturally

What do you enjoy doing that others find boring, even frustrating?

_____

_____

_____

When you read the newspaper or a magazine, what ideas or concepts draw your attention?

_____

_____

_____

What activities or interests are you most passionate about? What makes you purr?

_____

_____

_____

What are things you do naturally that you assumed everyone else did and discovered that was untrue?

_____

_____

_____

What are the common themes you see?

_____

_____

_____

Assuming success were assured, what would you do in life?

_____

_____

_____

II. Be Curious and Find the Right Niche

What are some opportunities you see in your work environment?

_____

_____

_____

What do your customers want that they aren't receiving?

_____

_____

_____

How can you "think outside the box" regarding a product or service you provide or are thinking of providing?

_____

_____

_____

If resources were not an issue, how could you improve your product or service?

_____

_____

_____

What's shifting in your marketplace?

_____

_____

_____

What are you doing to deliver a unique mix of value?

_____

_____

_____

_____

If you traveled 20 years into the future, what trends or innovations would you see? What sounds? Sights? Smells? Tastes? Feelings?

_____

_____

_____

_____

III. Make the Leap

What do you want to do next that presents you with the greatest challenge?

_____

_____

_____

_____

What keeps you from leaping?

_____

_____

_____

_____

What do you consider a new height?

_____

_____

_____

_____

What would ensure a safe landing "on all fours?"

_____

_____

_____

IV. Follow Your Instincts

How do you know when you're following your instincts? How does it feel?

_____

_____

_____

What keeps you from following your instincts or intuitions?

_____

_____

_____

Is there a common pattern or theme?

_____

_____

_____

When you're faced with difficult decisions, how do you usually handle them?

_____

_____

_____

How much would you say intuition plays in your decision-making? How much more would you want it to play?

_____

_____

_____

How do you picture yourself feeling when you've made a good decision and listened to the "meowing within?"

_____

_____

_____

_____

V. Clean Your Litter Box

List all the "things" that you hold on to from the past and why.

_____

_____

_____

What stands in the way of your opening a new chapter in your life?

_____

_____

_____

What are some of the ways that you could start anew?

_____

_____

_____

List the areas and how you plan to "start fresh."

_____

_____

_____

VI. Sit in the Window and Watch

When you step back and look at your work, what do you observe?

_____

_____

_____

If you were explaining your work to someone from another planet, how would you describe it?

_____

_____

_____

What are the workplace or life issues that agitate you the most?

_____

_____

_____

Which ones bring you the most contentment?

_____

_____

_____

Which aspects of your business or life take the most emotional energy?

_____

_____

_____

How can you restructure your environment to reduce stress and increase your energy?

_____

_____

_____

_____

If you were helping a friend or associate sort out your top three business issues, how would you approach them?

_____

_____

_____

_____

Is it any different from how you're handling them yourself?

_____

_____

_____

_____

VII. Meander and Explore

When was the last time you meandered and explored a new way of doing something? What did you do? What did you learn?

_____

_____

_____

If you had the time, what new business or career opportunity would you pursue?

_____

_____

_____

List some of the things you make judgments about.

_____

_____

_____

What would happen if you were willing to let those judgments go?

_____

_____

_____

How are you judging yourself and your performance on the job?

_____

_____

_____

Is there a better way to measure your progress? List some.

_____

_____

_____

_____

What are some of the new paths you might take to bring more excitement into your work and your life?

_____

_____

_____

VIII. Take Naps

When was the last time you took a catnap? How did you feel afterwards?

_____

_____

_____

Do you ever record your dreams? If so, what have you learned about yourself?

_____

_____

_____

When you daydream, what are some of the ideas you come up with?

_____

_____

_____

Take a catnap. When you get up, brainstorm at least five things you could do to improve your business or career.

_____

_____

_____

What things or situations block your progress?

_____

_____

_____

Think of the areas where you're "stuck." Take a nap. List any ideas you get while napping. (Don't be afraid to be "outrageous.")

_____

_____

_____

IX. Be Purrsistent

What are your values?

_____

_____

_____

What criteria do you use when assessing a goal or direction?

_____

_____

_____

How do you see these criteria relating to the values you've listed?

_____

_____

_____

What opportunities have you walked away from that didn't meet your standards? Why?

_____

_____

_____

Is there anything that keeps you from being purrsistent about your preferences?

_____

_____

_____

X. Wash Often

What are you currently doing to renew your body?

_____

_____

_____

Your mind?

_____

_____

_____

Your spirit?

_____

_____

_____

What would you like to be doing that you're not?

_____

_____

_____

_____

List what you see as the basic pleasures in life.

_____

_____

_____

_____

How will you make time to enjoy some of these pleasures in your daily life?

_____

_____

_____

_____

XI. Groom Those Who Groom You

Are you currently helping anyone "look their best?" What are you doing?

_____

_____

_____

Have you ever had a teacher or mentor who supported your career or personal growth? What are some of the things that they did?

_____

_____

_____

Brainstorm a list of ways you might support others in their work life.

_____

_____

_____

Which of these would you be willing to do in the next month?

_____

_____

_____

XII. Focus While Hunting

What are the things that distract you the most?

_____

_____

_____

What is your vision for yourself? For your business? (Where do you see yourself going in the next five to ten years?)

_____

_____

_____

If you had to pick one big overriding goal that supports your vision, what would it be?

_____

_____

_____

_____

How much time and concentration are you willing to devote to this overriding goal? What are some of the ways you can do this?

_____

_____

_____

_____

What kind of activities support your vision?

_____

_____

_____

What are some of the key strategies you can use to keep yourself and your business focused on your overriding goal?

_____

_____

_____

XIII. Balance Skillfully

List some of the opportunities or goals you would like to accomplish in the following areas:

Physical

_____

_____

_____

_____

Business/Career

_____
_____
_____
_____

Financial

_____
_____
_____
_____

Family/Relationship

_____
_____
_____
_____

Intellectual/Personal Development

_____
_____
_____
_____

Spiritual

_____
_____
_____
_____

Describe an ideal day for you.

_____
_____
_____

Describe an ideal week for you.

_____

_____

_____

_____

Describe an ideal month for you.

_____

_____

_____

_____

Describe your ideal life.

_____

_____

_____

_____

A business consultant, speaker, author, and trainer, Mary Hessler heads Mary Hessler & Associates (MHA), an organizational development consulting firm. MHA's purpose is simple: "commitment to the development of people and organizations." She also serves as Executive Director of *Inc. Magazine's Eagles CEO Program*, where she provides one-on-one consulting and roundtable facilitation to entrepreneurs of fast-growing companies. Dedicated to helping entrepreneurs succeed and their organizations grow, Hessler works with leaders in areas such as strategic planning and strategy development, visioning, organizational change, and group facilitation.

AUTHOR
Mary Hessler, Ph.D.

She consults on a range of subjects including entrepreneurship, leadership in the 21st century, team development and customer service.

Previously a principal with a major human resource consulting firm and the former vice president of a publicly traded training and development company, she is a member of the National Speakers Association, Organizational Development Network, SearchNet, American Society for Training and Development's Senior Forum, and Leadership Florida.

Hessler received her Ph.D. from the University of Virginia and her B.S. from the University of Massachusetts.

ILLUSTRATOR
Dino Kotopoulis

New Yorker Kotopoulis is an award-winning artist. An animation director, designer, and character sketcher for prestigious companies including Universal Studios, Depatie-Freleng, Disney, Leo Burnett, Foote Cone & Belding, J. Walter Thompson, and other major advertising agencies, Kotopoulis won a *Cleo* for his work on Charlie the Tuna commercials.

Kotopoulis studied at Pratt, The New York School of Visual Arts, and the Kyoto Art Center in Japan. He also taught at the Ontario School of Art in Toronto. A self-described "funny designer," Kotopoulis has a studio in Safety Harbor, Florida.

In 1992, he turned his artistic talents to wood, carving whimsical bas-relief caricatures of real people into furniture which he calls "Egos."